LST

D0192739

cupcakes

PEGGY PORSCHEN

PHOTOGRAPHY BY
GEORGIA GLYNN SMITH

Quadrille
PUBLISHING

'To my little
cupcake Max'

CONTENTS

MARBLE
CAKE

SCRUMPTIOUS
CARROT
cupcakes

VANILLA
CHIFFON
cupcakes

BLACK
FOREST

STICKY

PEGGY'S PARLOUR AND THE CUPCAKES

I am delighted to introduce my cutest little book to date, *Cupcakes*. This book shares a truly scrumptious selection of my favourite cupcake recipes; each baked and served at the Peggy Porschen Parlour in London's Belgravia. With twenty-five recipes included, there is a cupcake suited to every occasion – from classic summer pudding flavours such as Eton Mess and Lemon Meringue, to timeless autumnal favourites like Toffee Apple and Spiced Pumpkin. I wanted to make each recipe as accessible as possible, while maintaining my cupcakes' famous gourmet flavours. All of the ingredients included are available to buy from good supermarkets and the methods are straightforward and in no way intimidating – making them perfectly suited to home bakers of all levels. Even if you are unable to visit my Parlour regularly, I hope that this book will allow you to enjoy a little slice of Peggy Porschen whenever you might fancy it!

Baking has always been my passion; I find it the best therapy and it evokes wonderful childhood memories of baking with my mum at home in Germany. I hope that you take as much pleasure in baking, decorating and, most importantly, tasting the cupcakes as I have and that this book will become an invaluable source of inspiration in your home for many years to come.

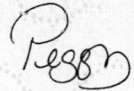

BAKING HINTS AND TIPS

ingredients

• For best results, use good-quality ingredients such as free-range eggs, proper unsalted butter (not margarine) and good-quality extracts (not essence).

• Soft cake flour is important for a good texture – don't be tempted to use a strong flour such as bread flour as it will make the sponge tough.

• All your ingredients should be at room temperature unless the recipe states otherwise. If needed, you can use the defrost setting on the microwave to gently soften the butter, and uncracked whole eggs can be gently warmed in a bowl of tepid water for 10 minutes.

timings and temperatures

• These are only guidelines. Bear in mind that ovens can vary greatly in their accuracy. The temperatures stated are for conventional ovens, so you will need to lower the temperature by 10–15°C if using a fan-assisted oven.

• Generally speaking, you get a more even rise from cupcakes if you bake them on the lower shelf of the oven.

• Turn the tins around halfway through cooking to ensure even baking.

equipment

• Using good-quality baking tins and cupcake cases that are not too thin will make a difference to the finished cupcake. I use cases that are a little smaller than standard muffin-sized ones, so if you use the larger muffin cases you will only get around 18 cupcakes.

• How light and fluffy you make your cake batter will also affect how many cupcakes you can get from one batch – the lighter the batter, the higher the yield.

measurements

• Always use special measuring spoons, not just a teaspoon or tablespoon from the cutlery drawer! A measuring teaspoon is exactly 5ml and a tablespoon is 15ml, so if you don't have a tablespoon measure, just use 3 teaspoons.

• Unless the recipe states otherwise, you should always level the top of the spoon with a knife or your fingertip.

• Some of the recipes in this book use medium eggs, some large – on average a medium egg is 50g cracked weight and a large egg is 60g. If you have unequal egg sizes, then just calculate the total weight of egg you need, crack the eggs you do have and weigh the quantity.

CHOCOLATE HEAVEN

ingredients

105g unsalted butter, softened

285g light brown sugar

2 large eggs

180g plain flour

½ tsp baking powder

½ tsp bicarbonate of soda

A pinch of salt

8g cocoa powder

125g plain chocolate (minimum 53% cocoa solids), chopped

165ml milk

makes 24

Preheat the oven to 165°C/Gas mark 3 and line two 12-hole muffin trays with cases.

Place the butter and half the sugar in a bowl and cream until pale and fluffy. Beat the eggs in a jug and slowly mix into the butter mixture. Sift the flour, baking powder, bicarbonate of soda, salt and cocoa into the mixture. Stir until just combined.

Place the chocolate, milk and remaining sugar in a saucepan. Gently bring to the boil and stir until all the chocolate and sugar have dissolved. Slowly pour this into the batter and mix. Scrape the bowl to make sure it is well combined. Transfer to a jug right away and pour into the cases until two-thirds full.

Bake immediately for 15–20 minutes, depending on your oven. They are cooked when the tops spring back to the touch. If you insert a clean knife into the sponge, it should come out with a small amount of crumb sticking to it, as the texture should be slightly sticky and dense. Let rest in the tray for a few minutes before removing and placing on a wire rack to cool completely.

to decorate
Use the chocolate cream cheese frosting on page 60 and top with white chocolate drops.

variation
For Chocolate Vanilla Cupcakes: Make the cupcakes following the recipe above and use the vanilla cream cheese frosting on page 59. Top with dark chocolate buttons.

Rich and creamy, this award-winning cupcake is pure heaven! For a lighter contrast, use a vanilla cream cheese frosting.

This is the Parlour's most popular cupcake. Its pudding-like texture makes it the perfect comfort food for cold and rainy autumn days.

STICKY TOFFEE

ingredients

290g dried dates, chopped

240ml boiling water

Seeds of ½ vanilla pod or 1½ tsp vanilla extract

290g self-raising flour

1½ tsp bicarbonate of soda

130g unsalted butter, softened

240g Muscovado sugar

3 large eggs

145g walnuts, chopped and toasted

Approximately 200g dulce de leche or soft caramel (or make your own by boiling a can of sweetened condensed milk submerged in water for 4 hours)

60ml plain syrup (see page 63)

makes 24

Preheat the oven to 175°C/Gas mark 4 and line two 12-hole muffin trays with cases.

Place the dates in a bowl and pour over the boiling water. Soak for 30 minutes. Gently stir to break up and add the vanilla. Sift the flour and bicarbonate of soda into another bowl.

Place the butter and sugar in another bowl and cream until pale and fluffy. Whisk the eggs lightly in a jug and slowly add to the butter mix, beating continuously at high speed. If the mixture starts to separate beat in 2–3 tablespoons of flour before adding the rest of the egg. Once all the egg has been added, fold in the flour, dates and walnuts. Stir until just combined.

Using a piping bag or a tablespoon, fill the cases until two-thirds full. Bake for 20–22 minutes, depending on your oven. The tops should be golden brown and spring back to the touch. If in doubt, insert a knife into the centre; it should come out clean.

Let rest for a few minutes outside of the oven. Brush the tops with syrup while they are still warm. Remove them from the trays and place on a wire rack to cool. When cold, use a melon baller to scoop out a small hole in the middle of each. Fill with a spoonful of dulce de leche.

to decorate

Use the caramel cream cheese frosting on page 59 and top with a gilded walnut half.

This is my version of an American classic – the soft sponge paired with tangy cream cheese frosting is pure perfection.

RED VELVET

ingredients

120g unsalted butter, softened

320g caster sugar

½ tsp salt

Seeds of 1 vanilla pod or 1 tbsp vanilla extract

2 large eggs

275g plain flour

2 tbsp cocoa powder

260g buttermilk

7 tsp (1 x 38ml bottle) red liquid food colouring

1½ tsp white wine vinegar

1¼ tsp bicarbonate of soda

makes 24

Preheat the oven to 175°C/Gas mark 4 and line two 12-hole muffin trays with cases.

Place the butter, sugar, salt and vanilla in a bowl and cream until pale and fluffy. Lightly beat the eggs in a jug and slowly add to the butter mixture while beating quickly. If the mixture starts to separate or curdle, stop adding the egg and beat in 2–3 tablespoons of flour. This will rebind the batter.

In a separate bowl, sift together the flour and cocoa. In a jug mix the buttermilk and food colouring. Mixing on low speed, add half the flour mix to the cake batter, followed by half the buttermilk, then the remaining flour and lastly the rest of the buttermilk. Be careful not to over-mix the batter. In a small bowl, mix together the vinegar and bicarbonate of soda. Fold this quickly but lightly through the cake batter. Using a piping bag or tablespoon, fill the cases until two-thirds full.

Bake for 15–20 minutes, depending on your oven. They are cooked when the tops look dry and spring back to the touch. If in doubt, insert a knife or skewer into each sponge; it should come out clean. Leave to cool a little in the tray before placing on a wire rack to cool completely.

to decorate

Use the vanilla cream cheese frosting on page 59 and top with some red velvet cupcake crumbs.

CHOCOLATE RASPBERRY HEART

ingredients

105g unsalted butter, softened

285g light brown sugar

2 large eggs

180g plain flour

A pinch of salt

½ tsp baking powder

½ tsp bicarbonate of soda

8g cocoa powder

125g plain chocolate (minimum 53% cocoa solids), chopped

165ml milk

250g raspberries

makes 24

Preheat the oven to 170°C/Gas mark 4 and line two 12-hole muffin trays with cases.

Place the butter and half the sugar in a bowl and cream until very pale and fluffy. Lightly whisk the eggs in a jug and slowly beat into the butter mixture. Sift the flour, salt, baking powder, bicarbonate of soda and cocoa powder into the batter and mix until just combined.

Place the chocolate, milk and the remaining sugar into a saucepan. Gently bring to the boil and stir until the chocolate and sugar have dissolved. Slowly pour the hot chocolate into the batter and mix. Scrape the bowl to make sure it is well combined. Transfer to a jug and, while it is still warm, fill the cases until two-thirds full. Drop 2–3 raspberries into each.

Bake immediately for 15–20 minutes, depending on your oven. They are cooked when the tops are slightly dry and spring back to the touch. If in doubt, insert a clean knife or skewer into the middle of each, it should come out with a small amount of crumb sticking to it. Leave them to cool a little in the tray before placing on a wire rack to cool completely.

to decorate
Use the chocolate cream cheese frosting on page 60 and top with sugarcraft hearts or lips.

Bake these for your sweetheart, but make extra for yourself! The combination of raspberries and chocolate is simply irresistible.

A sophisticated cupcake, this is perfect when served with a glass of pink Champagne in the British summer.

STRAWBERRY & CHAMPAGNE

ingredients

225g unsalted butter, softened

225g caster sugar

A pinch of salt

Seeds of 1 vanilla pod or 1 tbsp vanilla extract

4 medium eggs

225g self-raising flour

60ml Champagne syrup (see page 63)

About 250g Peggy's Strawberry & Champagne Jam or good-quality strawberry jam

makes 24

Preheat the oven to 175°C/Gas mark 4 and line two 12-hole muffin trays with cases.

Place the butter, sugar, salt and vanilla in a bowl and cream until pale and fluffy. Whisk the eggs lightly in a jug and slowly add to the butter mixture while beating quickly. If the mixture starts to separate or curdle, stop adding the egg and beat in 2–3 tablespoons of flour. This will rebind the batter. Once all the egg has been incorporated, sift in the flour and fold until just combined. Using a piping bag or tablespoon, fill the cases until two-thirds full.

Bake for 15–20 minutes, depending on your oven. The cupcakes are cooked when the tops are golden brown and spring back to the touch. If in doubt, insert a clean knife or skewer into each sponge; it should come out clean.

Once cooked, let them rest for a few minutes outside of the oven. Brush the tops with the syrup while they are still warm. Remove from the trays and leave to cool on a wire rack. When they are cold, hollow out a small hole in the middle of each with a melon baller and fill with the jam.

to decorate

Use the champagne cream cheese frosting on page 60 and top with a bonbon.

LEMON & RASPBERRY

ingredients

225g unsalted butter, softened

225g caster sugar

A pinch of salt

Finely grated zest of 2 unwaxed lemons

4 medium eggs

225g self-raising flour

250g raspberries

60ml lemon syrup (see page 63)

makes 24

Preheat the oven to 175°C/Gas mark 4 and line two 12-hole muffin trays with cases.

Place the butter, sugar, salt and lemon zest in a bowl and cream until pale and fluffy. Lightly whisk the eggs in a jug and slowly add to the butter mixture while beating quickly. If the mixture starts to separate or curdle, stop adding the egg and beat in 2–3 tablespoons of flour to rebind the mixture. Once all the egg has been incorporated, sift in the flour and fold until just combined. Using a piping bag or tablespoon, fill the cases until two-thirds full. Drop 2–3 raspberries into each cupcake.

Bake for 20–22 minutes, depending on your oven. The cupcakes are cooked when the tops are golden brown and spring back to the touch. If in doubt, insert a clean knife or skewer into each sponge; it should come out clean.

Leave the cakes to rest for a few minutes outside of the oven. Brush the tops with the syrup while they are still warm. Remove them from the trays and leave to cool completely on a wire rack.

to decorate
Use the lemon cream cheese frosting on page 60 and top with a fresh raspberry.

This is a very light and fluffy cupcake. The tart raspberries and lemons are balanced by the sweet and creamy frosting.

This is pure indulgence – far superior to the classic gâteau! The key is to use Griottine cherries for a plump, juicy and boozey finish.

BLACK FOREST

ingredients

105g unsalted butter, softened

285g light brown sugar

2 large eggs

180g plain flour

A pinch of salt

½ tsp baking powder

½ tsp bicarbonate of soda

8g cocoa powder

125g plain chocolate (minimum 53% cocoa solids), chopped

165ml milk

350g Griottine cherries, in a jar of Kirsch syrup

60ml Kirsch syrup (see page 63)

makes 24

Preheat the oven to 170°C/Gas mark 4 and line two 12-hole muffin trays with cases.

Place the butter and half the sugar in a bowl and cream until pale and fluffy. Lightly whisk the eggs in a jug and slowly add to the mixture. If it starts to separate or curdle, stop adding the egg and beat in 2–3 tablespoons of flour to rebind the batter. Sift the flour, salt, baking powder, bicarbonate of soda and cocoa powder into the batter and mix until just combined.

Place the chocolate, milk and the remaining sugar into a saucepan. Gently bring to the boil and stir until the chocolate and sugar have dissolved. Slowly pour the hot chocolate into the batter and mix. Scrape the bowl to make sure there are no lumps. Pour into a jug and, while it is still warm, fill the cases until two-thirds full. Drop 2–3 cherries into each.

Bake immediately for 15–20 minutes, depending on your oven. They are cooked when the tops are slightly dry and spring back to the touch. If in doubt, insert a clean knife or skewer into each, it should come out with a small amount of crumb sticking to it. Leave to rest in the trays for a few minutes outside of the oven and brush the tops with the syrup. Remove from the trays and leave to cool completely on a wire rack.

to decorate
Use the cherry cream cheese frosting on page 60 and top with a whole cherry and some chocolate sprinkles.

VANILLA CHIFFON

ingredients

225g unsalted butter, softened

225g caster sugar

A pinch of salt

Seeds of ½ vanilla pod or 1½ tsp vanilla extract

4 medium eggs

225g self-raising flour

60ml vanilla syrup (see page 63)

makes (24)

Preheat the oven to 175°C/Gas mark 4 and line two 12-hole muffin trays with cases.

Place the butter, sugar, salt and vanilla in a bowl and cream until pale and fluffy. Lightly beat the eggs in a jug and slowly add to the butter mixture while beating quickly. If the mixture starts to separate or curdle, stop adding the egg and beat in 2–3 tablespoons of flour to rebind the mixture. Once all the egg has been added, sift in the flour and fold until just combined. Using a piping bag or tablespoon, fill the cases until two-thirds full.

Bake for 15–20 minutes, depending on your oven. The cupcakes are cooked when the tops are golden brown and spring back to the touch. If in doubt, insert a clean knife or skewer into each sponge; it should come out clean. Leave them to rest for a few minutes in the tray and brush the tops with the syrup while they are still warm. Remove the cupcakes from the trays and leave to cool completely on a wire rack.

to decorate
Use the vanilla cream cheese frosting on page 59 and top with white metallic sugar pearls.

The beauty of this cupcake lies in the simplicity and purity of flavours. It is delightfully light, fluffy and creamy.

Packed with strawberries and topped with a wonderfully creamy frosting, this will have you dreaming of Wimbledon...

STRAWBERRIES & CREAM

ingredients

225g unsalted butter, softened

225g caster sugar

A pinch of salt

Seeds of 1 vanilla pod or 1 tbsp vanilla extract

4 medium eggs

240g self-raising flour

300g fresh strawberries, finely diced

60ml strawberry syrup (see page 63)

makes 24

Preheat the oven to 175°C/Gas mark 4 and line two 12-hole muffin trays with cupcake cases.

Place the butter, sugar, salt and vanilla in a mixing bowl and cream together until pale and fluffy. Whisk the eggs lightly in a jug and slowly add to the butter mixture while beating quickly. If the mixture starts to separate or curdle, stop adding the egg and beat in 2–3 tablespoons of flour to rebind the mixture. Once all the egg has been added, sift in the flour and fold until just combined.

Place a teaspoonful of the mix into the bottom of each case, then fold the strawberries into the rest of the batter. Using a piping bag or tablespoon, fill the cases until two-thirds full. Bake for 20–22 minutes, depending on your oven. The tops should be lightly browned and spring back to the touch. If in doubt, insert a knife into the centre of each; it should come out clean.

Once cooked, let rest for a few minutes outside of the oven. Brush the tops with syrup while they are still warm. Remove from the trays and leave to cool completely on a wire rack.

to decorate

Use an ice-cream scoop to top the cupcakes with a spoonful of the fridge-cold vanilla mascarpone frosting on page 60 and top with half a strawberry.

BANOFFEE

225g unsalted butter, softened

225g caster sugar

A pinch of salt

Seeds of 1 vanilla pod or 1 tbsp vanilla extract

4 medium eggs

225g self-raising flour

75g plain chocolate (minimum 53% cocoa solids), chopped

200g dulce de leche or soft caramel (or make your own by boiling a can of sweetened condensed milk submerged in water for 4 hours)

60ml vanilla syrup (see page 63)

makes 24

Preheat the oven to 175°C/Gas mark 4 and line two 12-hole muffin trays with cases.

Place the butter, sugar, salt and vanilla in a bowl and cream until pale and fluffy. Lightly beat the eggs in a jug and slowly add to the butter mixture while beating quickly. If the mixture starts to separate or curdle, stop adding the egg and beat in 2–3 tablespoons of flour. This will rebind the batter. Once all the egg has been incorporated, sift in the flour and fold until just combined. Fold in the chocolate. Using a piping bag or tablespoon, fill the cases until two-thirds full.

Bake for 15–20 minutes, depending on your oven. The cupcakes are cooked when the tops are golden brown and spring back to the touch. If in doubt, insert a clean knife or skewer into each sponge; it should come out clean.

Leave them in the trays and rest for a few minutes outside of the oven. Brush the tops with the syrup while they are still warm. Remove from the trays and leave to cool on a wire rack. When cold, use a melon baller to hollow out a small hole in each cupcake and fill with a spoonful of dulce de leche.

to decorate

Use the banana cream cheese frosting on page 59 and top with a slice of dried banana and chocolate sprinkles.

A firm favourite at the parlour, this delicious recipe is an ingenius fusion of a banana split and a banoffee pie.

PECAN PIE

ingredients

260g self-raising flour

2 tsp baking powder

200g soft light brown sugar

½ tsp salt

100g unsalted butter, softened

4 tbsp maple syrup

75g instant custard powder

150g whole milk

3 medium eggs

70ml brandy

75g vegetable oil

Seeds of 1 vanilla pod or 1 tbsp vanilla extract

150g pecans, chopped and toasted

80ml maple glaze (see page 63)

makes 24

Preheat the oven to 170°C/Gas mark 4 and line two 12-hole muffin trays with cases.

Place the flour, baking powder, sugar, salt, butter, maple syrup and custard powder into a large bowl and slowly mix together until resembling breadcrumbs. In a jug, whisk the milk, eggs, brandy, oil and vanilla until combined. Gradually pour this into the flour mix while beating on a medium speed. Make sure you add the liquid gradually or you will get lumps in the batter. Once you have added all of the liquid, fold through 100g of the pecans. Using a piping bag or tablespoon, fill the cases until two-thirds full. Sprinkle the tops with the remaining pecans.

Bake on a low shelf for 20–22 minutes, depending on your oven. They are cooked when the tops are golden brown and spring back to the touch. If in doubt, insert a knife or skewer into the centre of each; it should come out clean.

As soon as they are cooked, prick them all over with a skewer and brush the tops with the glaze. Remove from the trays and place on a wire rack to cool.

to decorate
Use the maple cream cheese frosting on page 59 and top with a few whole pecans.

This cupcake is rich in both taste and texture. Toast the pecans for more flavour and to add the perfect amount of crunch.

This is a lighter version of our award-winning carrot cake. It has just as much flavour and the pineapple adds depth and moisture.

CARROT & WALNUT

ingredients

270ml sunflower oil

360g light brown sugar

4 medium eggs, 2 of them separated

290g grated carrots (about 2 large carrots)

150g pineapple, finely chopped

140g walnuts, chopped and toasted

290g plain flour

½ tsp baking powder

½ tsp bicarbonate of soda

1½ tsp ground cinnamon

A pinch of salt

60ml of lemon syrup (see page 63)

makes 24

Preheat the oven to 175°C/Gas mark 4 and line two 12-hole muffin trays with cases.

Beat the oil and sugar until well mixed and slightly aerated. In a separate bowl, whisk the 2 whole eggs and 2 egg yolks, then add this gradually to the oil and sugar, beating on high speed. Fold the carrots, pineapple and nuts into the mixture using a metal spoon. Sift together the flour, baking powder, bicarbonate of soda and cinnamon and fold this into the batter.

In a separate clean, dry bowl, whisk the egg white with the salt until soft peaks form. Mix a third of the egg white into the batter until well combined and then gently fold in the remaining egg white. Using a piping bag or tablespoon, fill the cases until two-thirds full.

Bake for 20–22 minutes, depending on your oven. The cupcakes are cooked when the tops are golden brown and spring back to the touch. If in doubt, insert a clean knife into the centre of each; it should come out clean.

Brush the tops with the syrup while still warm. Once just warm, remove from the trays and leave to cool on a wire rack.

to decorate
Use the lemon cream cheese frosting on page 60 and top with sugarcraft carrots.

ETON MESS

ingredients

225g unsalted butter, softened

225g caster sugar

A pinch of salt

Seeds of 1 vanilla pod or 1 tbsp vanilla extract

4 medium eggs

240g self-raising flour

250g Peggy's Summer Berry Jam or other good-quality berry jam

60ml vanilla syrup (see page 63)

makes 24

Preheat the oven to 175°C/Gas mark 4 and line two 12-hole muffin trays with cases.

Place the butter, sugar, salt and vanilla in a bowl and cream until pale and fluffy. Beat the eggs in a jug and slowly add to the butter mixture while beating quickly. If the mixture starts to separate or curdle, stop adding the egg and beat in 2–3 tablespoons of flour to rebind the mixture. Once all the egg has been added, sift in the flour and fold until just combined.

Fill one side of a piping bag with jam and the other side with batter and fill the cases until two-thirds full. Bake for 15–20 minutes, depending on your oven. The cupcakes are cooked when the tops are lightly browned and spring back to the touch. If in doubt, insert a clean knife into the centre of each; it should come out clean.

Leave them to rest for a few minutes outside of the oven. Brush the tops with the syrup while still warm. Remove from the trays and leave to cool completely on a wire rack.

to decorate
Stir some crushed raspberries through the vanilla mascarpone frosting on page 60. Pipe over the frosting and finish with a meringue kiss and a raspberry.

Topped with a fresh and creamy raspberry frosting and a meringue kiss, this is the taste of summer in a cupcake!

Inspired by my German origins, this 'apfelstrudel' cupcake is incredibly moist and is flavoured with nuts, fruits and spices.

APPLE STRUDEL

ingredients

75g sultanas

25ml Calvados or brandy

3 medium eggs

250g caster sugar

A pinch of salt

Finely grated zest of
1 unwaxed lemon

110ml vegetable oil

400g Bramley apples,
peeled and finely chopped
(approx 4 apples)

80g hazelnuts, chopped
and toasted

280g self-raising flour

40g ground hazelnuts
or almonds

1½ tsp ground cinnamon

½ tsp ground cloves

½ tsp ground nutmeg

A pinch of ground ginger

1 tsp baking powder

60ml Calvados syrup (see
page 63)

makes 24

Soak the sultanas in the Calvados, ideally several days in
advance but at least overnight.

Preheat the oven to 175°C/Gas mark 4 and line two 12-hole
muffin trays with cases.

Place the eggs, sugar, salt and lemon zest into a bowl and whisk
immediately on a high speed until light, fluffy and doubled in
volume. Keeping the speed on high, gradually pour the oil into
the mix in a thin steady stream, whisking constantly to obtain a
smooth emulsion. Add the apples and hazelnuts and lightly fold.
Sift the remaining dry ingredients into the mixture and gently
fold until combined. Using a piping bag or a tablespoon, fill the
cases until three-quarters full.

Bake for 20–22 minutes, depending on your oven. The tops
should be golden brown and spring back to the touch. If in
doubt, insert a knife into each; it should come out clean.

Leave to rest in the trays for a few minutes outside of the oven.
Brush the tops with the syrup while they are still warm. Remove
from the trays and leave to cool completely on a wire rack.

to decorate

Use the Calvados and cinnamon cream cheese frosting on page
60 and sprinkle over some chopped and toasted hazelnuts.

GIANDUJA

ingredients

225g unsalted butter, softened

225g light brown sugar

A pinch of salt

150g self-raising flour

50g ground hazelnuts

25g cocoa powder

1½ tsp baking powder

4 medium eggs

50g hazelnuts, chopped and toasted

60ml plain syrup (see page 63)

120g chocolate-hazelnut spread

makes 20

Preheat the oven to 175°C/Gas mark 4 and line two 12-hole muffin trays with 20 cases.

Place the butter, sugar and salt in a mixing bowl and cream until pale and fluffy. Sift the flour, ground hazelnuts, cocoa powder and baking powder into a separate bowl. Beat the eggs in a jug and slowly add to the butter mixture while beating quickly. If the mixture starts to separate or curdle, stop adding the egg and beat in 2–3 tablespoons of flour to rebind the mixture. Once all the egg has been added, add the dry ingredients and hazelnuts, folding until just combined.

Using a piping bag or tablespoon, fill the cases until two-thirds full. Bake for 15–20 minutes, depending on your oven. The tops should look dry and spring back to the touch. If in doubt, insert a knife into the centre of each; it should come out clean. Rest for a few minutes outside of the oven and brush with the syrup. Remove from the trays and leave to cool on a wire rack.

When cold, use a melon baller to hollow out a small hole in the middle of each and fill with the chocolate-hazelnut spread.

to decorate

In a heatproof bowl over a saucepan of simmering water, gently warm the chocolate-hazelnut ganache on page 62 until dipping consistency. Dip in the cupcakes so that the tops are covered and finish with a gilded hazelnut.

Hazelnut and chocolate is a match made in heaven. The dipped liquid ganache adds a lovely smooth and glossy finish.

SALTED CARAMEL

ingredients

225g unsalted butter, softened

225g caster sugar

A pinch of salt

Seeds of 1 vanilla pod or 1 tbsp vanilla extract

4 medium eggs

225g self-raising flour

60ml vanilla syrup (see page 63)

200g dulce de leche or soft caramel (make your own by boiling a can of sweetened condensed milk submerged in water for 4 hours)

1½ tsp fine sea salt

makes 24

Preheat the oven to 175°C/Gas mark 4 and line two 12-hole muffin trays with cases.

Place the butter, sugar, salt and vanilla into a bowl and cream until pale and fluffy. Lightly beat the eggs in a jug and slowly add to the butter mixture while beating quickly. If the mixture starts to separate or curdle, stop adding the egg and beat in 2–3 tablespoons of flour to bring it back together. Once all the egg has been added, sift in the flour and fold until combined. Using a piping bag or tablespoon, fill the cases until two-thirds full.

Bake for 15–20 minutes, depending on your oven. They are cooked when the tops are golden brown and spring back to the touch. If in doubt, insert a clean knife or skewer into each sponge; it should come out clean.

Let them rest for a few minutes outside of the oven. Brush the tops with the syrup while they are still warm. Remove from the trays and leave to cool completely on a wire cooling rack.

Mix together the dulce de leche and sea salt. When the cupcakes are cold, hollow out a small hole in the middle of each using a melon baller and fill with the salted caramel.

to decorate
Use the salted caramel cream cheese frosting on page 59 and top with chunks of toffee or a sprinkling of sea salt.

Grown-up candy in a cupcake form! Use proper sea salt flakes such as Maldon or Fleur de Sel – it will make a world of difference to the flavour.

This captures all the classic flavours of the iconic dessert: creamy mascarpone, dark chocolate and a really good kick of coffee!

TIRAMISU

makes 24

Preheat the oven to 175°C/Gas mark 4 and line two 12-hole muffin trays with cases.

Place the butter, sugar, salt, vanilla and espresso in a mixing bowl and cream together until pale and fluffy. Beat the eggs lightly in a jug and slowly add to the butter mixture while beating quickly. If the mixture starts to separate or curdle, stop adding the egg and beat in 2–3 tablespoons of flour before adding the rest of the egg. This will rebind the batter. Once all the egg has been added, sift in the flour and fold until just combined. Using a piping bag or tablespoon, fill the cases until two-thirds full.

Bake for 15–20 minutes, depending on your oven. The tops should be golden brown and spring back to the touch. If in doubt, insert a knife into the centre; it should come out clean.

Once cooked, let rest for a few minutes outside of the oven and brush with the syrup while they are still warm. Remove from the trays and place on a wire rack. When they are cold, hollow out a small hole in the middle of each using a melon baller and fill with a spoonful of ganache.

to decorate
Use the coffee mascarpone frosting on page 60 and dust with cocoa powder.

TOFFEE APPLE

ingredients

225g unsalted butter, softened

225g light brown sugar

A pinch of salt

Seeds of 1 vanilla pod or 1 tbsp vanilla extract

4 medium eggs

240g self-raising flour

250g Bramley apples, peeled and chopped (approx 2 large apples)

60ml vanilla syrup (see page 63)

makes 24

Preheat the oven to 175°C/Gas mark 4 and line two 12-hole muffin trays with cupcake cases.

Place the butter, sugar, salt and vanilla in a mixing bowl and cream together until pale and fluffy. Beat the eggs lightly in a jug and slowly add to the butter mixture while beating quickly. If the mixture starts to separate or curdle, stop adding the egg and beat in 2–3 tablespoons of flour before adding the rest of the egg. This will rebind the mixture. Once all the egg has been added, sift in the flour and fold until the batter is just combined. Fold in the apple. Using a piping bag or tablespoon, fill the cases until two-thirds full.

Bake for 20–22 minutes, depending on your oven. They are cooked when the tops are golden brown and spring back to the touch. If in doubt, insert a clean knife or skewer into the centre of each; it should come out clean.

Once cooked, let rest for a few minutes outside of the oven. Brush the tops with syrup while they are still warm. Remove them from the trays and place on a wire rack to cool completely.

to decorate
Use the caramel cream cheese frosting on page 59 and finish with a lollipop stick.

Ever wondered what to bake for a bonfire night party? Well this cupcake is it – tart apple cupcakes with a sweet caramel frosting.

The mulled wine jam we stock in the Parlour at Christmas makes the ideal festive filling but you can use a spiced berry jam.

MULLED WINE

ingredients

225g unsalted butter, softened

225g caster sugar

A pinch of salt

Finely grated zest of 2 unwaxed oranges

240g self-raising flour

1 tsp ground cinnamon

¼ tsp ground nutmeg

¼ tsp ground cloves

4 medium eggs

2 tbsp red wine

60ml mulled wine syrup (see page 63)

120g Peggy's Mulled Wine Jam or other good-quality berry jam

makes 24

Preheat the oven to 175°C/Gas mark 4 and line two 12-hole muffin trays with cases.

Place the butter, sugar, salt and zest in a bowl and cream until pale and fluffy. Sift the flour and spices into a separate bowl. Beat the eggs lightly in a jug and slowly add to the butter mixture while beating quickly. If the mixture starts to separate or curdle, stop adding the egg and beat in 2–3 tablespoons of flour to rebind the mixture. Once all the egg has been added, stir in the red wine. Add the flour and fold until just combined.

Using a piping bag or tablespoon, fill the cases until two-thirds full. Bake for 15–20 minutes, depending on your oven. They are cooked when the tops are lightly browned and spring back to the touch. If in doubt, insert a knife or skewer into the centre of each, it should come out clean.

Once cooked, let rest for a few minutes outside of the oven. Brush the tops with the syrup while they are still warm. Remove from the trays and leave to cool completely on a wire rack. Once cold, use a melon baller to hollow out a small hole in the middle of each cupcake and fill with the jam.

to decorate
Use the orange and Cointreau™ frosting on page 60 and top with a piece of candied orange peel.

LEMON MERINGUE

ingredients

225g unsalted butter, softened

225g caster sugar

A pinch of salt

Finely grated zest of 3 unwaxed lemons

4 medium eggs

225g self-raising flour

60ml lemon syrup (see page 63)

120g good-quality lemon curd

makes 24

Preheat the oven to 175°C/Gas mark 4 and line two 12-hole muffin trays with cupcake cases.

Place the butter, sugar, salt and lemon zest in a mixing bowl and cream together until pale and fluffy. Beat the eggs lightly in a jug and slowly add to the butter mixture while beating quickly. If the mixture starts to separate or curdle, stop adding the egg and beat in 2–3 tablespoons of flour to rebind the mixture. Once all the egg has been added, sift in the flour and fold until the batter is just combined.

Using a piping bag or tablespoon, fill the cases until two-thirds full. Bake for 15–20 minutes, depending on your oven. They are cooked when the tops are lightly browned and spring back to the touch. If in doubt, insert a clean knife or skewer into the centre of each sponge; it should come out clean.

Once cooked, let them rest for a few minutes outside of the oven. Brush the tops with the syrup while they are still warm. Remove them from the trays and place on a wire rack. When they are cold, hollow out a small hole in the middle of each using a melon baller and fill with the lemon curd.

to decorate
Pipe over the meringue frosting on page 62 and quickly brown the top with a chef's blow torch or under a very hot grill.

Use the best-quality lemon curd you can buy (or, even better, make your own!) to add even more flavour to these zesty little cupcakes.

SUGAR PLUM

ingredients

225g unsalted butter, softened

225g caster sugar

A pinch of salt

Seeds of 1 vanilla pod or 1 tbsp vanilla extract

4 medium eggs

225g self-raising flour

6 plums, stoned and cut into small pieces

60ml vanilla syrup (see page 63)

makes 24

Preheat the oven to 175°C/Gas mark 4 and line two 12-hole muffin trays with cases.

Place the butter, sugar, salt and vanilla in a bowl and cream until pale and fluffy. Lightly beat the eggs in a jug and slowly add to the butter mixture while beating quickly. If the mixture starts to separate, stop adding the egg and beat in 2–3 tablespoons of flour. This will rebind the batter. Once all the egg has been added, sift in the flour and fold until just combined. Using a piping bag or tablespoon, fill the cases until two-thirds full. Top each with pieces of plum, pushing some of them into the batter.

Bake for 20–22 minutes, depending on your oven. The cupcakes are cooked when the tops are golden brown and spring back to the touch. If in doubt, insert a clean knife or skewer into each sponge; it should come out clean.

Once ready, let them rest for a few minutes outside of the oven and brush the tops with the syrup. Remove them from the trays and leave to cool completely on a wire rack.

to decorate
Use the cinnamon cream cheese frosting on page 59 and top with a sugarcraft snowflake.

This is a great alternative to serve at Christmas time – it is extremely simple and deliciously fruity.

Perfect for Halloween or Thanksgiving, this tastes exactly like a traditional pumpkin pie.

SPICED PUMPKIN

ingredients

100g unsalted butter, softened

280g pumpkin purée

½ tsp fine sea salt

115g buttermilk

325g light brown sugar

4 medium eggs

240g plain flour

2½ tsp baking powder

½ tsp bicarbonate of soda

¾ tsp ground ginger

1 tsp ground cinnamon

¾ tsp ground nutmeg

¼ tsp ground cloves

makes 24

Preheat the oven to 175°C/Gas mark 4 and line two 12-hole muffin trays with cases.

Melt the butter and leave to cool slightly. Place the pumpkin, salt, buttermilk and sugar in a large bowl and, by hand, use a balloon whisk to mix well. One at a time, add the eggs, whisking well between each addition.

Sift together the flour, baking powder, bicarbonate of soda and the spices. Lightly whisk the flour mix into the pumpkin mixture in two batches. Add the melted butter and gently incorporate until just mixed. Using a piping bag or tablespoon, fill the cases until two-thirds full.

Bake for 15–20 minutes, depending on your oven. The cupcakes are cooked when the tops are golden brown and spring back to the touch. If in doubt, insert a clean knife or skewer into each sponge; it should come out clean.

Let the cupcakes cool for a few minutes in their trays before placing on a wire rack to cool completely.

to decorate
Use the cinnamon cream cheese frosting on page 59 and top with a sugarcraft pumpkin.

Cupcakes and
cocktails go hand
in hand, and the
cosmopolitan lends
itself perfectly as
inspiration for
this recipe.

COSMO

ingredients

125g dried cranberries

3 tbsp Cointreau™ liqueur

225g unsalted butter, softened

225g caster sugar

A pinch of salt

Finely grated zest of 2 unwaxed oranges

4 medium eggs

225g self-raising flour

60ml orange and Cointreau™ syrup (see page 63)

makes 24

Soak the cranberries in the Cointreau™ liqueur, cover the bowl with clingfilm and leave to infuse overnight.

Preheat the oven to 175°C/Gas mark 4 and line two 12-hole muffin trays with cases.

Place the butter, sugar, salt and zest in a bowl and cream until pale and fluffy. Beat the eggs lightly in a jug and slowly add to the butter mixture while beating quickly. If the mixture starts to separate or curdle, stop adding the egg and beat in 2–3 tablespoons of flour to rebind it. Once all the egg has been added, sift in the flour and fold until just combined. Using a piping bag or tablespoon, fill the cases until two-thirds full. Drain the cranberries, reserving the liquid (use this to make the syrup). Divide the cranberries evenly and drop into the cupcakes.

Bake for 15–20 minutes, depending on your oven. They are cooked when the tops are golden brown and spring back to the touch. If in doubt, insert a clean knife into each sponge; it should come out clean. Leave to rest for a few minutes outside of the oven and brush the tops with syrup. Remove them from the trays and leave to cool completely on a wire rack.

to decorate
Use the orange and Cointreau™ cream cheese frosting on page 60 and top with colourful sugar sprinkles.

PINK MARSHMALLOW

ingredients

225g unsalted butter, softened

225g caster sugar

A pinch of salt

Seeds of 1 vanilla pod or 1 tbsp vanilla extract

4 medium eggs

225g self-raising flour

A little pink food colouring

50g mini marshmallows

60ml vanilla syrup (see page 63)

makes 24

Preheat the oven to 175°C/Gas mark 4 and line two 12-hole muffin trays with cases.

Place the butter, sugar, salt and vanilla in a bowl and cream together until pale and fluffy. Beat the eggs lightly in a jug and slowly add to the butter mixture while beating quickly. If the mixture starts to separate or curdle, stop adding the egg and beat in 2–3 tablespoons of flour to rebind the mixture. Once all the egg has been added, sift in the flour and fold until just combined. Stir in enough food colouring to create a light shade of pink and gently fold in the marshmallows.

Using a piping bag or tablespoon, fill the cases until two-thirds full. Make sure that all of the marshmallows are completely covered by the batter. Bake for 15–20 minutes, depending on your oven. They are cooked when the tops are lightly browned and spring back to the touch. If in doubt, insert a clean knife or skewer into the centre of each; it should come out clean.

Once cooked, immediately remove them from the trays to prevent the marshmallow from sticking and place on a wire rack. While they are still warm, brush the tops with the syrup. Leave to cool completely.

to decorate
Pipe over the pink marshmallow frosting on page 62.

Unapologetically sweet, this is every little girl's dream cupcake! For a boy's party, colour the sponge and frosting blue instead.

GINGERBREAD

ingredients

250ml semi-skimmed milk

Finely grated zest and juice of 1 unwaxed orange

150g light brown sugar

A large pinch of salt

300g golden syrup

150g dark treacle

4 tsp ground ginger

4 tsp ground cinnamon

2 tsp ground allspice

180g unsalted butter, chilled and cut into pieces

1 tsp bicarbonate of soda

350g self-raising flour

3 medium eggs

60ml plain syrup (see page 63)

N.B. Allspice is not the same as mixed spice.

makes 24

Preheat the oven to 170°C/Gas mark 4 and line two 12-hole muffin trays with cases.

Add enough milk to the orange juice to make up 300ml of liquid. Place the milk mixture in a saucepan with the zest, sugar, salt, golden syrup, treacle and spices and gently bring to the boil, stirring constantly. Remove from the heat and add the butter, stirring with a whisk until melted.

Sift the flour and bicarbonate of soda into a large bowl and add the slightly cooled liquid mix. Mix gently with a whisk. Add the eggs one at a time and mix them through, until the cake batter is just smooth and thoroughly combined. Pour the mixture into a jug and fill the cases until three-quarters full.

Bake for 20–22 minutes, depending on your oven. They are cooked when they are well-risen and spring back to the touch. If in doubt, insert a knife into the centre; it should come out clean.

Once baked, let rest for a few minutes outside of the oven. Brush the tops with syrup while they are still warm. Remove from the trays and leave to cool completely on a wire rack.

to decorate
Use the lemon cream cheese frosting on page 60 and top with a little gingerbread man biscuit.

Dark, moist and spicy, the flavour of this cupcake develops over time and is therefore even better when eaten the next day.

BASIC CREAM CHEESE FROSTING

250g full-fat cream cheese, slightly softened
250g unsalted butter, softened
625g icing sugar, sifted

Place the cream cheese in a bowl and beat until smooth and creamy.

Place the butter and a third of the sugar into a separate bowl and cream until very pale and fluffy. Add another third of the sugar and repeat. Add the remaining sugar and beat again, scraping the sides of the bowl to ensure no lumps remain. Add the cream cheese, a little at a time, and mix at a low speed until combined. Chill until firm enough to pipe.

TIP: When adding a liquid to taste, add only a little bit at a time to make sure that the frosting doesn't become too runny.

variations

Vanilla
Add ½ the seeds of a vanilla pod or 1½ tsp vanilla extract.

Caramel
Gently mix in 150g soft caramel or dulce de leche.

Salted Caramel
Gently mix in 150g soft caramel or dulce de leche and 1 tsp of fine sea salt.

Maple
Add 4 tbsp dark maple syrup.

Cinnamon
Add 1½ tsp ground cinnamon.

Banana
Gently mix in 60g banana purée.

(variations continued on page 60)

CREAM CHEESE FROSTING

variations (continued)

Lemon
Add the finely grated zest of 2 unwaxed lemons.

Cherry
Add 4 tbsp kirsch syrup drained from a jar of Griottine cherries and a small amount of pink food colouring.

Champagne
Add Marc de Champagne to taste and a little pink food colouring.

Orange & Cointreau™
Add the finely grated zest of 2 oranges and flavour to taste with Cointreau™.

Calvados & Cinnamon
Add 1½ tsp ground cinnamon and Calvados (or French brandy) to taste.

Chocolate
Using 200g full-fat cream cheese, 200g unsalted butter and 500g sifted icing sugar, make up the Basic Cream Cheese Frosting (see page 59). Gently mix in 280g Chocolate Ganache (see page 62).

MASCARPONE FROSTING

200g unsalted butter, softened
500g icing sugar
300g mascarpone, slightly softened

Place the butter and half of the sugar in a bowl and cream together on a high speed until very pale and fluffy. Add the remaining sugar with the mascarpone and beat on medium speed, scraping down the sides of the bowl to ensure no lumps remain. Beat until the mix is smooth, but do not over-beat or the mixture will become runny. If necessary, chill until firm enough to pipe.

variations

Vanilla
Add ½ the seeds of a vanilla pod or 1½ tsp vanilla extract.

Coffee
Add 1 tsp espresso powder or instant coffee.

CHOCOLATE GANACHE

150ml whipping cream
20g glucose
200g dark chocolate (minimum 53% cocoa)

Place the cream and glucose in a saucepan and bring to a bare simmer. Place the chocolate in a heatproof bowl and pour over the hot cream. Sit for 30 seconds to let the chocolate melt, then stir with a balloon whisk until smooth and shiny. Leave to set at room temperature; it should be the consistency of soft butter.

variation

Chocolate-Hazelnut
Using 100ml whipping cream, 15g glucose, 65g dark chocolate and 65g milk chocolate make up the Chocolate Ganache as above. Stir through 65g chocolate-hazelnut spread while still warm. Use straight away for dipping or leave to set.

MERINGUE FROSTING

100g pasteurised liquid egg white
Juice of ½ lemon
3 tbsp water
A pinch of salt
260g caster sugar

Place the egg white, lemon juice, water and salt into a clean, dry bowl and whisk until aerated and soft peaks form. Lower the speed and add a third of the sugar, 1 tbsp at a time, then raise the speed and beat well for a minute. Lower the speed again and repeat with the next third of sugar. Add the remaining sugar in the same way, then put the speed up to high and beat well for at least 3–4 minutes, or until fluffy, white and firm.

Use immediately. Do not store the frosted cupcakes in the fridge as the humidity will melt the meringue.

variation

Pink Marshmallow
Add 2 tbsp of water instead of 3, and add 2 tsp of vanilla extract. Whisk in a few drops of pink liquid food colouring at the end for a light pink frosting.

PLAIN SYRUP

60ml water
60g caster sugar

Place the water and sugar into a small saucepan and bring just to the boil. Stir until the sugar crystals have all dissolved, then remove from the heat. Set aside to cool.

TIP: Always brush the syrup over the cupcakes whilst they are still warm. This way the syrup is absorbed into the whole cupcake.

variations

Vanilla
Add ½ a used vanilla pod while cooking or ½ tsp vanilla extract to the cooled syrup.

Strawberry
Add 50g diced strawberries to the water and sugar and bring to the boil. Strain the syrup.

Coffee
Add 1 tsp espresso powder or instant coffee.

Kirsch
Add a little kirsch syrup (drained from a jar of cherries) and kirsch liqueur to taste.

Calvados
Use 30ml of lemon juice and 30ml of water instead of just water. Add Calvados to taste.

Lemon
Use 60ml of lemon juice instead of water.

Champagne
Flavour to taste with Marc de Champagne.

Orange & Cointreau™
Use 60ml of orange juice instead of water. Add Cointreau™ to taste.

Mulled Wine
Use 30ml of orange juice and 30ml of red wine instead of water and add a sachet of mulled wine spices to the pan and bring to the boil. Let infuse for 20 minutes before straining.

Maple Glaze
Place 20ml water, 65g unsalted butter, 60ml maple syrup and 60g caster sugar into a pan and bring just to the boil while stirring. Remove from the heat and add 2 tbsp brandy.

ACKNOWLEDGEMENTS

This book wouldn't have been possible without the enthusiasm and support of some incredible people. First, I would like to thank our very own Stephanie Balls for sparking the initial idea and overseeing the entire project from concept to creation. Well done, you are a star! I'd like to give a huge thank you to Marianne Stewart, pastry chef and baker extraordinaire, for developing the most delicious cupcake recipes and for meticulously test baking and perfecting each and every crumb. You are such a talent and I am delighted you agreed to help me with this book. As always, I can't thank my dream team enough: Jane O'Shea and Helen Lewis from Quadrille Publishing, Georgia Glynn Smith for yet another set of stunning pictures and Vicky Sullivan for the beautiful styling.

Editorial director **Jane O'Shea**
Creative director **Helen Lewis**
Editor **Louise McKeever**
Designers **Gemma Hogan, Nicola Ellis**
Photographer **Georgia Glynn Smith**
Stylist **Vicky Sullivan**
Recipe development **Marianne Stewart**
Production director **Vincent Smith**
Production controller **Sasha Taylor**

First published in 2013 by
Quadrille Publishing Ltd
Alhambra House
27–31 Charing Cross Road
London WC2H 0LS
www.quadrille.co.uk

Text, recipes and designs © 2013 Peggy Porschen
Photography © 2013 Georgia Glynn Smith
(except page 4 © Adam Ellis)
Artwork, design and layout © 2013 Quadrille
Publishing Ltd

British Library Cataloguing-in-Publication Data

A catalogue record for this book is available from the British Library.

ISBN: 978 184949 344 4

Printed in China